INDONESIA

LETTERS FROM AROUND THE WORLD

David Cumming

Photographs by Julio Etchart

CHERRYTREE BOOKS

LETTERS FROM AROUND THE WORLD

Distributed in the United States by
Cherrytree Books
1980 Lookout Drive
North Mankato, MN 56001

Library of Congress Cataloging-in-Publication Data
Cumming, David, 1953-
    Indonesia / David Cumming ; photographs by Julio
Etchart.
      p.cm. -- (Letters from around the world)
    Includes index.
    ISBN 1-84234-241-X (alk. paper)
    1. Indonesia--Juvenile literature. I. Etchart, Julio, 1950-
ill. II Title. III. Series.

DS615.C86 2004
959.8--dc22

2004041344

First Edition
9 8 7 6 5 4 3 2 1

First published in 2004 by
Evans Brothers Ltd
2A Portman Mansions
Chiltern Street
London W1U 6NR
Copyright © Evans Brothers Limited 2004

Conceived and produced by

Nutshell
MEDIA
www.nutshellmedialtd.co.uk

Editor: Polly Goodman
Design: Mayer Media Ltd
Cartography: Encompass Graphics Ltd
Artwork: Mayer Media Ltd
Consultants: Jeff Stanfield and Anne Spiring
All photographs were taken by Julio Etchart.

Printed in China.

Acknowledgments
The photographer would like to thank the MasRukhan
family, the staff and students of Seloliman School, East Java,
Indonesia, the staff at PPLH Ecotourism Centre, and Fiona
Smith from VSO, Indonesia, for all their help with this book.

Cover: Muhammad (center) with his friends (from the left)
Miftahul, Kholis, Agus, and Evi.
Title page: Some of Muhammad's friends enjoying a mid-
morning rice snack at school.
This page: A view over volcano craters in East Java. There
are 400 volcanoes in Indonesia.
Contents page: Muhammad's classmate Arti enjoys a rice
cracker at break time.
Glossary page: Writing answers on the blackboard in a
math lesson.
Further Information page: A farmer plows a rice field with
the help of two cows.
Index: Villagers from Biting on their way to work.

Contents

My Country

Wednesday, May 6

Biting
Trawas
East Java
Indonesia 61375

Dear Chris,

Selamat pagi! (pronounced "say-LAR-mart PAR-gee." This means "hello" in Indonesian.)

My name is Muhammad MasRukhan and I'm eight years old. I live in the village of Biting, in Indonesia. Biting is on a big island called Java. There are many islands in Indonesia.

Being your pen pal is a great idea. I can tell you all about life in Indonesia.

Write back soon!

From

Muhammad

This is me with my mom, dad, and my little sister, Rizki. She's four years old.

Indonesia is a long chain of islands between Malaysia and Australia. Some of the islands are too small to live on. Others are among the biggest in the world.

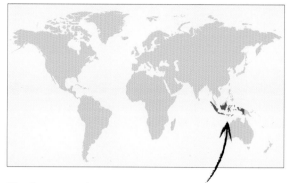

Indonesia's place in the world.

PHILIPPINES

THAILAND

South China Sea

BRUNEI

PACIFIC OCEAN

M A L A Y S I A

SINGAPORE

Kapuas

B o r n e o

Equator

Sumatra

Sulawesi

I N D O N E S I A

Puncak Jaya
16,484 ft (5,029 m)

Irian Jaya

Java Sea

JAKARTA

Bandung *Java* Surabaya
        Biting   *Bali*   *Flores*
        Malang

EAST TIMOR

Timor

INDIAN OCEAN

N

AUSTRALIA

0 200 400 600 800 kilometers

0   200   400 miles

There are more than 13,600 islands in Indonesia. They stretch from the Indian Ocean to the Pacific Ocean.

Indonesia has few large cities. Most people live in villages like Biting. They grow food crops such as rice, corn, or peanuts, or work on plantations growing mahogany trees. Mahogany wood is used to make furniture.

About 300 people live in Biting. The nearest city is Malang, 90 miles (150 km) away. It takes 90 minutes to get there by bus.

Overhead cables bring electricity to houses in Biting.

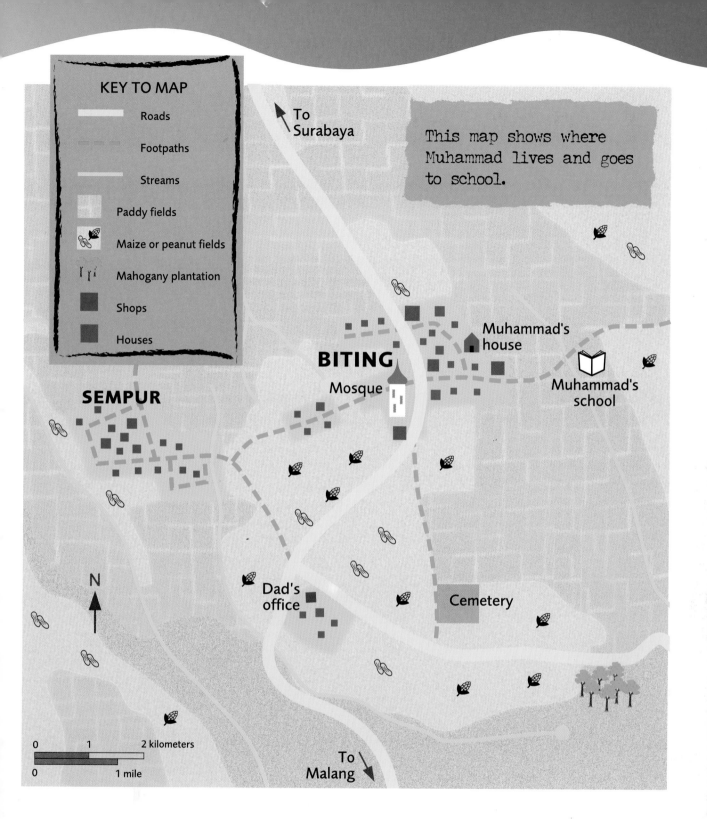

KEY TO MAP

Roads

Footpaths

Streams

Paddy fields

Maize or peanut fields

Mahogany plantation

Shops

Houses

To Surabaya

This map shows where Muhammad lives and goes to school.

BITING

SEMPUR

Mosque

Muhammad's house

Muhammad's school

N

Dad's office

Cemetery

0   1   2 kilometers

0   1 mile

To Malang

There is one road that runs through Biting. There are also many paths. Muhammad walks to school along a path through the fields. The village has four small grocery stores and a mosque.

Landscape and Weather

Java is like the rest of Indonesia. It has many forests, hills, and mountains, and little low or flat land. Many of the mountains are volcanoes.

Many of Indonesia's farmers dig flat terraces into the hillsides for growing rice.

Indonesia is on the Equator, so it is hot all year round. In East Java, the temperature can reach as high as 97 °F (36 °C). A wind called the monsoon brings a lot of rain between October and April. There is not much rain between May and September.

Mount Bromo is near Biting. It is an active volcano which still erupts.

Biting's Climate

January

Temperature
79 °F
(26 °C)

Rainfall
11–12 in
(300 mm)

July

Temperature
81 °F
(27 °C)

Rainfall
2–3 in
(64 mm)

At Home

Muhammad's home is similar to other houses in Biting. It has brick walls and a wooden roof. The roof sticks out on pillars to keep the house cool. The mosque (see page 27) also has a large roof to stop the inside from getting hot.

Muhammad and his family leave their shoes outside the house, which is the custom in Indonesia. It helps to keep the dirt out.

Muhammad's house is on one floor. It has a living room, a kitchen, a bathroom, and a small room for prayers. There are three bedrooms— one for Muhammad, one for his parents, and one for Rizki.

Muhammad's family has a TV and VCR in the living room, but they still spend a lot of time reading.

Laundry dries quickly in the hot Indonesian sun.

Muhammad's dad works hard looking after the garden and animals.

There is a garden in the back of the house. Muhammad's parents grow fruit and vegetables there. They also grow vegetables in a nearby shared garden.

The family owns three ducks and two chickens. Muhammad collects their eggs for his mom to cook.

Muhammad's mom grows spinach (on the left) and peanuts (on the right) in the garden.

Thursday, June 12

Biting
Trawas
East Java
Indonesia 61375

Dear Chris,

Thanks for your letter. It took over three weeks to get here. Our village isn't big enough to have a mail van, so Dad had to pick it up from Malang, which is 90 miles (150 km) away. All our mail is delivered to Malang. How do you get your letters?

I'm glad you like drawing. It's one of my favorite hobbies, too. We're learning how to draw maps at school. Today we drew the area around our houses. Tomorrow we're going to draw real maps of Biting. I'm practicing at home.

Write again soon!

From

Muhammad

Here I am drawing our house and the countryside around it.

Food and Mealtimes

Rice is the most important food in Indonesia. People eat it every day. It is used to make a popular dish called *nasi goreng* (pronounced "nar-SEE go-RENG"). The rice is stir-fried in a wok with meat, vegetables, and eggs. *Gado-gado* is another favorite. It's a salad covered with peanut sauce.

Every week, a food trader (in red) visits the village on her motorcycle to sell vegetables, tofu, and fish.

Muhammad's dad collects avocados from trees in the shared garden. He uses a net on a pole.

This village woman is peeling the shells from peanuts. The peanuts will be used in rice crackers, and to make sauces.

On street stalls you can buy barbecued lamb or chicken on skewers. They are dipped into a spicy shrimp paste, or sauces made from coconut milk, peanuts, or soybeans.

Dried carp is a favorite breakfast meal. Carp swim in the streams around Biting.

For breakfast, Muhammad has rice and fish. Lunch is more rice and fish, along with vegetables and tofu.

In the evening, the family eats stir-fried rice with the leftovers of the day's fish and vegetables.

Like most people in Indonesia, Muhammad's family does not have a table. They sit on the floor, instead.

Friday, July 18

Biting
Trawas
East Java
Indonesia 61375

Hi Chris,

If you like coconut, why don't you try making some coconut rice?

You will need: 1 cup coconut milk (fresh is best; otherwise canned),
4 tablespoons grated coconut (fresh if possible; dried if not),
$1/2$ cup long-grain rice, salt, and pepper.

1. Put the rice in a sieve and rinse it well with water.
2. Then put it in a saucepan with the coconut milk.
3. Bring to a boil and simmer for 10 minutes, or until most of the coconut milk has been absorbed.
4. Mix in the grated coconut and season with a little salt and pepper.

Try it and let me know what you think.

Muhammad

Here I am watching Mom stirring the coconut rice.

School Day

Muhammad's school is about a mile (2 km) from his home. Most students walk there from the villages nearby.

There are 120 students in the school, between 7 and 11 years old. They all have to wear the school uniform.

It takes Muhammad (left) and his friend Setiawan (center) about half an hour to get to school. They are joined by other pupils along the way.

This is Muhammad's class in front of the school sign. There are 29 pupils in his class.

PEMERINTAH KABUPATEN MOJOKERTO
DINAS PENDIDIKAN
SDN.SEI OLIMAN
KEC.TRAWAS

Each class lasts 40 minutes. The week's timetable is on the wall.

Muhammad only goes to school in the morning. His classes start at 8 A.M. There's a short break at 10:30 A.M. for a snack. School ends at 12:30 P.M., when Muhammad goes home for his lunch.

In math class, children work out answers on the board.

Muhammad's classmate Arti enjoys a rice cracker at break time.

Muhammad studies Indonesian, math, science, geography, and history. Once a week he also learns English.

There are three school terms and one month's vacation during the year.

Tuesday, August 19

Biting
Trawas
East Java
Indonesia 61375

Dear Chris,

Have I told you about our playground game? Everyone stands in a circle and one person throws a stone in the middle. Each person has to hop on one foot to the stone and back in 10 hops, then nine hops, then eight, down to one hop. The first person to put their other foot down is out.

What do you play in the playground? Write back and tell me.

From

Muhammad

Here's my class playing a game on the playground.

Off to Work

A farmer plows his paddy fields of rice near Biting.

More than half the people in Indonesia are farmers. They grow rice and other crops. In the cities there are new factories making stereos, computers, clothes, and shoes.

Villagers share a ride to work, where they are helping a farmer with his harvest.

Muhammad's dad works for an education center. He teaches people how to care for the land. He also teaches them to look after the forests. Huge areas of forest are being destroyed every year. Muhammad's dad is trying to stop this.

Here is Muhammad's dad in his office, with the people who work with him.

Free Time

Most people in Indonesia do not have lots of money. Many parents do not have enough money to buy electronic toys for their children. Muhammad is lucky. His parents have a TV and a VCR. When he's not watching TV, he likes to play soccer with friends.

Soccer is Muhammad's favorite sport. He plays with his friends around the village.

These are spectators at the soccer stadium in Malang. They are watching Arema, Muhammad's favorite team.

Wednesday, September 17

Biting
Trawas
East Java
Indonesia 61375

Hi Chris,

Your playground game sounds fun.

So, you're a judo whiz kid! Well, I'm the class arm-wrestling champion. Simply the best! No one comes near beating me. We probably do it a little differently here. Instead of locking hands, we lock wrists and then try to force the other person's hand to the ground. Try it some time. I bet I could beat you!

Bye

Muhammad

My friend Ali is strong, but not as strong as me.

Religion

Like most Indonesians, Muhammad and his family are Muslims. They follow the religion of Islam. After getting up, Muhammad washes and says his prayers. In the evening, too, he washes before praying and going to bed.

A drummer calls villagers to Friday prayers in the mosque.

This is Biting's mosque, the place where Muslims pray.

Friday is Islam's holy day. After school, Muhammad goes to the mosque to pray. Then he goes to the mosque's school. Here he learns Arabic, so that he can read the Qur'an. This is Islam's holy book.

Children read the Qur'an at the *madrasah* (the mosque's school).

Fact File

Capital City: Jakarta is in the west of Java. As well as the capital, Jakarta is Indonesia's biggest city.

Other Major Cities: Bandung and Surabaya.

Size: 737,830 square miles (1,919,440 km²). Indonesia is the fourth-largest country in the world. It has 13,677 islands. They stretch for 3,160 miles (5,100 km) through 3 million square miles (8 million km²) of sea, which means that there is more water than land in Indonesia.

Population: About 231 million. There are 362 different peoples in Indonesia.

Flag: The Indonesian flag has a red and a white band. Red stands for courage and white stands for purity.

History: The islands of Indonesia were once known as the Spice Islands. European merchants traveled there by ship to buy spices such as cloves and nutmegs.

Languages: Bahasa Indonesia is the official language, which is spoken throughout the country. Other important languages are English and Dutch. There are also 250 local languages, of which Javanese, Sundanese, Malay, and Madurese are the most spoken.

Currency: Rupiah (divided into sen). 1 rupiah = 100 sen.

Highest Mountain: Puncak Jaya 16,484 feet (5,029 m), in Irian Jaya.

Rainforest: Indonesia has the world's second-largest area of tropical rainforest. Only Brazil has a bigger area.

Wildlife: The rainforests are home to many different birds, and animals such as orangutans and lizards. The world's largest lizard lives on Komodo island. It can grow up to 10 feet (3 m) long and weigh 300 pounds (135 kg).

Longest River: The Kapuas, 708 miles (1,142 km), in Borneo.

Main Religions: Islam is the main religion in Indonesia. About 88 percent of the people follow it. Other people follow Christianity, Hinduism, and Buddhism.

Stamps: Indonesian stamps often show the country's festivals, wildlife, and plants.

Glossary

carp A small freshwater fish that lives in rivers and ponds.

corn Any grain crop grown for food.

Equator An imaginary line round the middle of the Earth. The weather is hot all year long there.

erupt To burst open. When a volcano erupts, it throws out lava, solid rocks, and gases from inside the earth.

harvest To collect a crop.

Islam The religion of Muslims.

monsoon The name given to a major wind that blows over Indonesia, bringing rain for several months each year.

mosque The building in which Muslims pray.

paddy field A field where rice is grown.

pillar A tall stone or wooden post that holds something up.

plantation A large area of land where one crop is grown to sell abroad.

Qur'an The holy book of Islam.

rice cracker A big cracker made from puffed rice.

temperature How hot or cold something or someone is.

terrace A flat piece of ground on the side of a hill, like a step.

tofu A food made from soybeans.

volcano A mountain with a hole in the top. It can erupt, throwing out lava and ash through the hole.

wok A deep saucepan with a round bottom. It is used for frying food quickly.

Further Information

Information books:

Merrell, Leila. *Continents: Asia.* Heinemann, 2002.

Guile, Melanie. *Culture In: Indonesia.* Heinemann, 2003.

Hegedus, Umar. *Keystones: Muslim Mosque.* A&C Black, 2000

Martin, Fred. *Step Into Indonesia.* Heinemann Library, 1998.

Hollyer, Beatrice. *Wake up World!.* Henry Holt, 1999.

McCulloch, Julie. *A World of Recipes: Indonesia.* Heinemann, 2003.

Senker, Cath. *A Year of Religious Festivals: My Muslim Year.* Hodder & Stoughton Children's Division, 2003.

Resource Packs:

"Global Topics" (Unicef, 2002): large color photos, photocopiable topic books, and a teacher's guide for looking at aspects of daily life in Indonesia.

Web sites:

CIA World Factbook
www.cia.gov/
Facts and figures about Indonesia and other countries.

Indonesian Home Page
http://indonesia.elga.net.id/
Information about all things Indonesian, including recipes, clothes, and traditional games.

Index

Numbers in **bold** refer to photographs or illustrations.